CHEROKEE

OCT 1 1 1990

# The Marshall Cavendish Library of Science Projects

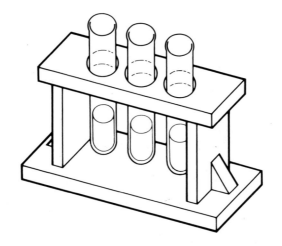

## Marshall Cavendish Corporation

London • New York • Toronto

# The Marshall Cavendish
# SCIENCE PROJECT BOOK
## *of*
# THE EARTH

## Written by Steve Parker
## Illustrated by David Parr

**Reference Edition published 1989**

The Marshall Cavendish Library of Science projects
The Earth Volume 5

© Marshall Cavendish Limited MCMLXXXVI
© Templar Publishing Limited MCMLXXXV
Illustrations © Templar Publishing Limited MCMLXXXV

Trade edition published by Granada Publishing Limited

Reference edition published by:
  Marshall Cavendish Corporation
  147 West Merrick Road
  Freeport
  Long Island
  NY 11520

Printed and bound in Italy
by L.E.G.O. s.p.a., Vicenza

**Library of Congress Cataloging in Publication Data**

The Marshall Cavendish Library of Science Projects

  Includes index.
  Contents: (1) Water
  1. Science – Experiments – Juvenile Literature.
2. Science – Juvenile Literature. (1. Science –
Experiments. 2. Experiments) 1. Marshall Cavendish
Corporation.
Q164.M28   1986   507.8   86-11731
ISBN 0-86307-624-6 (Set)

ISBN 0-86307-629-7 (Vol 5 The Earth)

PICTURE CREDITS
*Pages 4-5:* Tony Stone Photo Library, London
*Pages 10-11:* Science Photo Library/S. Summerhays
*Pages 16-17:* Science Photo Library/David Parker
*Page 19:* Science Photo Library/Dr Harold Rose
*Pages 20-21:* Tony Stone Photo Library, London
*Pages 22-23:* Science Photo Library/Jon Wilson
*Pages 26-27:* Science Photo Library/David Parker
*Pages 28-29:* Science Photo Library/David Parker
*Pages 32-33:* Science Photo Library/Martin Dohrn
*Pages 38-39:* Science Photo Library/Richard Folwell;
*tl* JCB Sales Ltd.
*Page 41:* Science Photo Library/Earthsat.

# CONTENTS

Science is all about discovering more about your world, finding out why certain things happen and how we can use them to help us in our everday lives. SCIENCE PROJECTS looks at all these things. It's packed with exciting experiments and projects for you to do, and fascinating facts for you to remember. It will teach you more about the world around you and to understand how it works.

# IN THE BEGINNING...

**F**or centuries before the advent of modern science, people had very different ideas about the Earth from those we have today.

Before Ferdinand Magellan's ships sailed round the globe in 1519-22, and Francis Drake did the same in 1577-80, many people believed the world was flat. They thought that if you sailed too close to the edge, you simply fell off! Nowadays men have seen our ball-shaped planet from space and have even measured its diameter to the nearest few yards.

In about 1650 Archbishop James Usher of Ireland worked out that God had created the Earth at 9 o'clock on the morning of 23 October, 4004 BC. He used the Bible and other religious books to calculate this date. But modern science tells us that the Earth is about 4,600 million years old – over one million times older than Usher's estimate.

In fact, the Earth is so big and so old that it is difficult for us to imagine its vastness. For instance, if the tallest building in the world (the Sears Tower in Chicago, USA, which reaches 1,454 feet or 443 meters) was reduced to only a fraction of an inch in height, in proportion the Earth would still measure over 100 feet (about 30 meters) across. And if you shortened the Earth's age to just one day (24 hours) its history would read something like this.

At 12.00 midnight the planet would just be forming from a cloud of whirling gases condensing in space. At 5.30 am the first rocks would form. About 8.30 am the first traces of life appear – bacteria and simple algae in the seas.

It would not be until 9:00 pm that evening that the more complicated creatures – like fish and crabs – evolve in the oceans, and it would take until about 11.00 pm for the dinosaurs to be walking the Earth. We humans would not appear until one minute before

midnight, and the whole of civilization as we know it would not even fill the last second before the end of the day!

Our planet and our civilization seem so permanent and real and huge that we cannot imagine them being much different from the way they are today.

But in reality, the Earth is really only one small planet circling our Sun. And the Sun itself is just an average star, and only one of billions and billions in the vastness of the Universe. We are really but a speck in space, and no more than a blink in the passing of time.

**5**

# UNDER YOUR FEET

Cutting through the Earth is like cutting through a giant apple. On the outside is a thin skin which is called the *crust.* The Earth's crust is thinner, though, in proportion to the apple's skin.

Underneath the crust is the *mantle,* a thick layer much like the flesh of an apple. And at the center of both the Earth and the apple is the *core.* Of course, we haven't yet discovered whether there are any pits in the Earth.

## The crust

The crust takes up less than 1% of the Earth's volume. It varies in depth: under the sea it is about 3mi (5 kms) thick, but under the land it is about 22mi (35kms) thick. At the base of the crust is a special zone known as the Mohorovičić discontinuity (or Moho for short) which is named after the Yugoslavian geologist who discovered it in 1909. In the Moho there is a sudden change from the relatively light rocks of the crust to the heavier, denser rocks of the mantle.

## The mantle

This makes up 83% of the Earth's volume. It is about 1,800 mi (2,900km) thick and the deeper you go, the more dense and heavy the rocks from which it is made become. At the base of the mantle is another zone, the Gutenberg discontinuity, where the

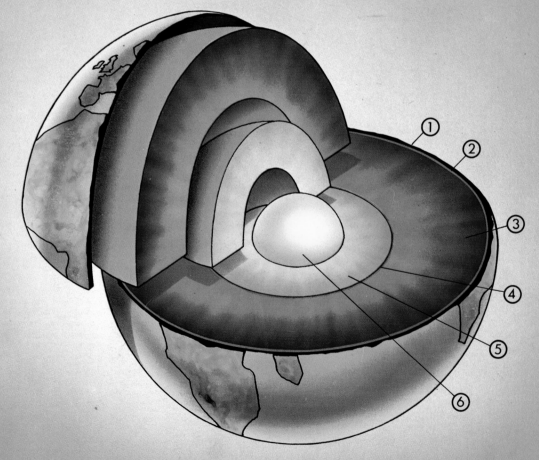

heavy rocks and metals of the mantle suddenly give way to even heavier metals of the core.

## The core

Metals such as iron and nickel, combined with oxygen, make up the core of our planet. This takes up 16% of the Earth's volume. Deep in the core the pressure is over 4 million times stronger than the atmospheric pressure at the surface, and the temperature is about 7,200°F (4,000°C). So when you see adventure films about expeditions to the center of the Earth, as a scientist you will know they are simply far-fetched stories.

## How do we know what's inside?

The deepest hole drilled into the Earth goes about 7½ mi (12kms) into the crust, which is not even halfway through its 'skin'. Because of this, most of the information about what is deep beneath our feet comes from the study of earthquakes and their shock waves – a branch of science called *seismology*.

Shock waves from an earthquake travel through the Earth like sound waves through the air. But the shock waves move at different speeds, and are bent (refracted) or bounced back (reflected) depending on the substance they are going through. Seismologists record tremors from one earthquake, or from a big explosion, at different places on the Earth's surace. Depending on where the shock waves come up, and at which angle they emerge, and how long they have taken, we can make scientific guesses as to what is inside the Earth.

### 1 Crust
*Varies in thickness from 3 mi (5 kms) under oceans to 22 mi (35 kms) or more underland. Makes up less than 1% of the Earth's volume and 0.5% of its weight. Oceanic crust is made mainly of silicon, magnesium, iron, aluminum and calcium, combined in various ways with oxygen. The continental crust is chiefly silicon and aluminum combined with oxygen. Temperature at the base of the crust is around 698 – 752°F (370 – 400°C).*

### 2 Moho
*The zone where the rocks at the base of the crust give way to the heavier rocks of the mantle. Density change: 1.7 to 1.9 oz per cubic in (2.9 to 3.3 grams per cubic centimetre).*

### 3 Mantle
*About 1,800 mi (2,900 kms) thick. Makes up 83% of the Earth's volume and 67% of its weight. The mantle is mostly silicon, magnesium and iron combined with oxygen. Temperature ranges from 1472°F (800°C) in outer mantle to 4532°F (2,500°C) at base of mantle.*

### 4 Gutenberg
*The zone where the rocks at the base of the mantle give way to the heavier metals and other substances of the core. Density change: 3.2 to 5.9oz per cubic inch 5.5 to 10 grams per cubic centimeter).*

### 5 Outer core
*1305 mi (2,100 kms) thick. Together with the inner core, this makes up 16% of the Earth's volume and 32% of its weight. Probably liquid; mainly iron and nickel.*

### 6 Inner core
*About 746 mi (1,200 kms) radius. Probably solid – 90% iron and 10 nickel combined with oxygen. The center of the Earth is 3960 mi (6,371 kms) from the surface. The temperature there is about 5400 – 7200°F (3,000 – 4,000°C) and the pressure over 4 million atmospheres.*

# Science factfile

## The amazing Earth!

**Age** 4,600 million years (the same as other planets in our Solar System).
**Diameter** (12,756 kms) 7928 mi at the Equator and (12,713 kms) 7901 mi from the North Pole to the South Pole. This means the Earth is not a perfect sphere – in fact, it's slightly pear-shaped.

**Circumference** (40,075 kms) 24,907 mi at the Equator. At an average walking speed it would take you 10 months non-stop to walk round the Earth.
**Area** 196,975,135 sq mi (510,165,600 sq kms), of which 71% is made up of oceans.
**Volume** Over (765 million cubic yds) 1 million million cubic kms.

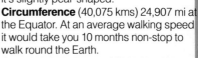

**Weight** Almost 6,000 million million million tons.
**Rotation** The Earth spins once every 23 hours, 56 minutes and 4 seconds. Leap years make up for the lost time so clocks can stay at 24 hours per day.

**Surface speed** If you stood on the Equator you would effectively be moving at over 1,000 mph (1,600 kms per hour) because, of course, our planet is constantly rotating on its axis. What's more, the Earth is also rushing through space on its orbit round the Sun at 67,000 mph (108,000 kms per hr).

# WORLDWIDE JIGSAW

Did you know that the Atlantic Ocean is becoming wider by ¾in (2 cms) each year? Or that one day America will collide with Asia? In fact, did you realize that the map of the world is constantly changing?

Such movements are the result of *plate tectonics*. This theory says that the Earth's surface is made up of about about six large slabs or plates, plus many smaller ones. The plates are curved to match the Earth's spherical surface and fit together like a giant jigsaw.

But the jigsaw does not stay still. All the time the plates are slowly moving. Over millions of years the continents drift across the globe. Mountains and valleys are formed where the plates crumple into each other or pull apart. Volcanoes erupt through the cracks, and earthquakes quake as the plates rub past each other. In fact, the theory of plate tectonics helps to explain a lot about why the surface of the Earth looks and behaves as it does. It is an excellent example of a scientific theory that brings together many events and processes in one simple explanation.

## What's a 'plate'?

Each of the Earth's plates is 60 miles (about 100 kms) or more thick, which is much thicker than the crust. In fact, each plate is made up of two layers: crust on the outside, and a layer of mantle beneath. All together the plates form a stiff shell, 60mi (100 kms) thick all around the Earth. This is called the *lithosphere*. Beneath the lithosphere is the rest of the mantle, called the *asthenosphere.* This is thought to be 'plastic' or semi-liquid in nature, so that the rigid lithosphere plates float and move about on its surface. There are three main types of joint between plates, as you can see in the diagrams below.

## The driving force

So how do the plates move, you may ask? Well, it's thought that the top 311 miles (500 kms) of mantle beneath the plates are not still either. Instead the material from which they're made flows to and fro and up and down due to convection currents set up by the tremendous temperatures and pressures deep within the Earth. In some areas, mantle material is forced up nearer the surface, into the gap between two plates. This usually happens beneath the sea. As it cools the mantle material forms rock that adds on to the edge of the plate, pushing it sideways.

## How plates join

Here you can see three types of joint between the Earth's plates.

**1** When two oceanic plates push into each other under the sea, one plate bends under the other. This forms a valley on the ocean floor called a *deep-sea trench.* The other plate crumples and cracks at its edge, forming a mountain range with volcanoes. If the mountains are high enough they will poke above the sea's surface to make a chain of islands. *(Example:* Japan.)
**2** Continental plates are thicker than oceanic ones. When the two collide, the oceanic plate bends underneath. The edge of the continental plate is lifted and rumpled into a coastal

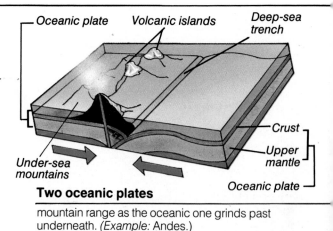

Oceanic plate — Volcanic islands — Deep-sea trench — Crust — Upper mantle — Oceanic plate — Under-sea mountains

**Two oceanic plates**

mountain range as the oceanic one grinds past underneath. *(Example:* Andes.)

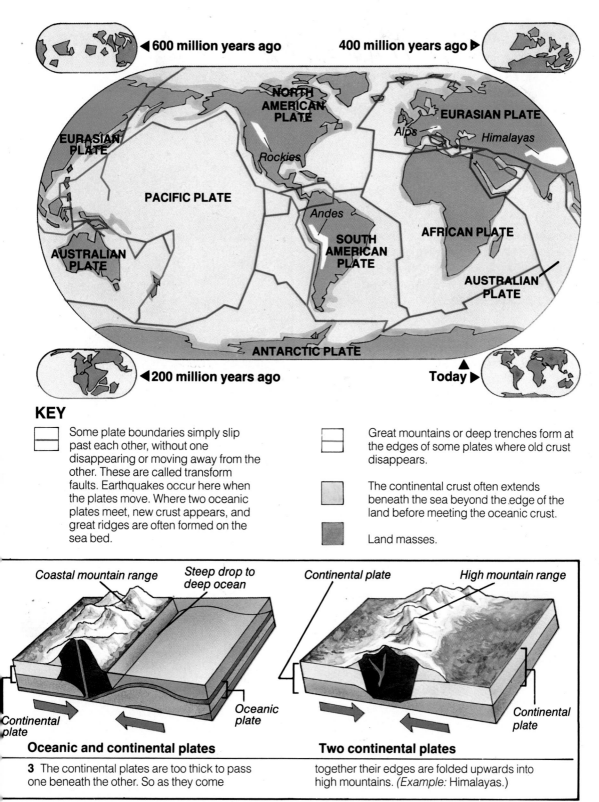

◄ **600 million years ago**

**400 million years ago** ►

NORTH AMERICAN PLATE

EURASIAN PLATE

Alps

Himalayas

EURASIAN PLATE

*Rockies*

PACIFIC PLATE

*Andes*

SOUTH AMERICAN PLATE

AFRICAN PLATE

AUSTRALIAN PLATE

AUSTRALIAN PLATE

ANTARCTIC PLATE

◄ **200 million years ago**

**Today** ►

## KEY

Some plate boundaries simply slip past each other, without one disappearing or moving away from the other. These are called transform faults. Earthquakes occur here when the plates move. Where two oceanic plates meet, new crust appears, and great ridges are often formed on the sea bed.

Great mountains or deep trenches form at the edges of some plates where old crust disappears.

The continental crust often extends beneath the sea beyond the edge of the land before meeting the oceanic crust.

Land masses.

*Coastal mountain range*

*Steep drop to deep ocean*

*Continental plate*

*High mountain range*

*Continental plate*

*Oceanic plate*

*Continental plate*

**Oceanic and continental plates**

**Two continental plates**

**3** The continental plates are too thick to pass one beneath the other. So as they come

together their edges are folded upwards into high mountains. *(Example: Himalayas.)*

**9**

# SHAKING & QUAKING!

The Earth's crust is constantly moving, as we have seen on the previous pages. Most of the movements are slow and gradual, but occasionally there is a sudden, violent movement. If you bend a twig too far, it snaps – and rocks do the same. The sudden release of pent-up stresses and strains in the Earth's crust causes the ground to shudder as shock waves spread through the land and oceans. We know these shivers and shakes as *earthquakes*.

## Quakes and plates

Many earthquakes happen along the borders of the vast plates that make up the Earth's lithosphere (page 8). The plates try to move past each other but friction holds them back until, suddenly,

### How earthquakes happen

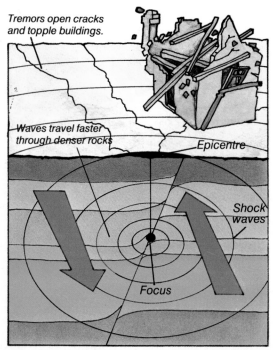

Tremors open cracks and topple buildings.

Waves travel faster through denser rocks

Epicentre

Shock waves

Focus

*Hellfire erupts from Kilauea volcano in Hawaii. This spectacular display of the Earth's power occurs*

they slip many yards in one go.

There are probably 2,000 or more earthquakes every day over the whole world, but most of these are so small that they are hardly detectable. Strong quakes occur about once every two weeks, and most of these happen deep in the ocean floor. Severe earthquakes in areas where many people live are thankfully rare. In 1956 an earthquake in Shenshi, China, killed over 800,000 people. In 1964 a strong earthquake in Alaska lifted parts of the land over 16 yards (15 metres). Few people lived in the region however, and

*when molten rock bursts out through a weak spot in the Earth's crust.*

the quake comes from is called the *focus*. If this is under the ground, the point directly above it on the surface is called the *epicenter*.

## Violent volcanoes

Another sudden and spectacular display of the Earth's power can be seen in the eruption of a volcano. Fluid rock, called *magma* while deep in the crust, bursts out through a hole and flies into the air as *lava*. Rocks and ash can be thrown many miles and the lava flows down the sides of the volcano. As it hardens into *igneous* rock, this lava makes the volcano's cone higher and wider. Volcanoes, along with fissures (where the lava flows out of a long crack instead of a hole) are responsible for making large amounts of igneous rocks in the Earth's crust. There are about 500 active volcanoes on the Earth's continents, plus many more beneath the sea. When a volcano has not erupted for many years we say it is *dormant.*

there were only 114 deaths.

Seismologists are the scientists who study earthquakes and the plate movements producing them. Using satellite observations and modern 'tilt meters' based on laser beams, they can sometimes detect tiny movements of the crust that indicate an earthquake is building up. Hopefully in the future this can be done with great accuracy so that warnings will be given in time to allow people to leave the area.

Some earthquakes happen at or near the Earth's surface, but others have their origin deep underground. The place where

**Inside a volcano**

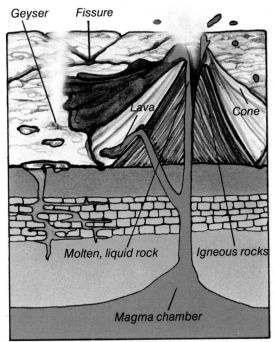

Geyser  Fissure

Lava

Cone

Molten, liquid rock   Igneous rocks

Magma chamber

# POLES APART

Did you know that there are really two North Poles? One is the geographic North Pole. This is the point where the Earth spins on its *axis*. If you stood there for a whole day you would effectively turn right around once. To find the second North Pole, however, you would need to hold a compass flat so that the 'N' end of its needle swings around to point north. Then you'd have to follow the direction of the needle across the frozen seas of the Arctic icecap. You'd eventually come to a place where the needle would swing wildly round and round, not pointing in any one direction. You would then be at the North Pole – but not the geographic one, which is hundreds of miles away. This one is called the *magnetic* North Pole.

A compass needle is a small bar magnet that swings around to line up with the lines of magnetic force in and around the Earth. The scientist remembers that, with magnets, like poles repel and unlike poles attract. The 'N' end of the compass needle is really its south pole, which is pulled towards the Earth's North Pole.

But why does the Earth have a magnetic field? It's thought that the solid crust and outer mantle spin round at a different speed to the heavy inner core. Now, the core is made mostly of metal, while the

**DYNAMO THEORY**
*Metal-containing mantle and crust spin at a different speed to metal-rich inner core, so acting as a dynamo. This produces an electric current in the core, and a magnetic field in and around the Earth.*

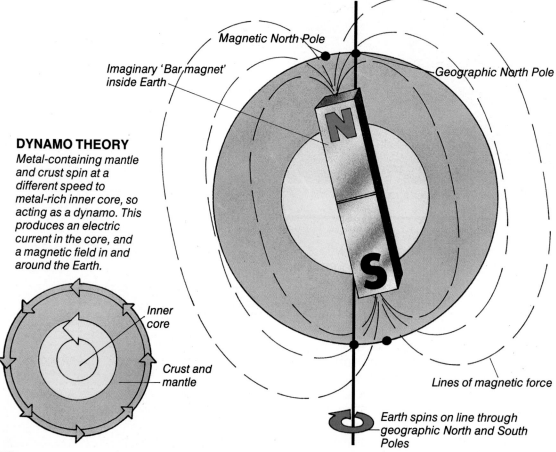

Magnetic North Pole

Imaginary 'Bar magnet' inside Earth

Geographic North Pole

N

S

Inner core

Crust and mantle

Lines of magnetic force

Earth spins on line through geographic North and South Poles

mantle also contains plenty of metallic rocks. So these two metallic layers, one moving past the other, act like a dynamo to create a magnetic field. (They also create electric currents in the core.) It's as though the Earth had a giant bar magnet inside it.

The Earth's magnetic field is tilted 11° away from the axis on which the Earth spins. This is why the geographic North Pole is so far from the magnetic North one. And on the underside of the Earth there are two South Poles as well, one geographic and one magnetic.

## The wandering poles

Certain rocks have tiny magnetic particles in them, such as mineral crystals containing iron. As a molten rock solidifies, the particles from which it is formed line up like tiny compass needles, pointing north and south. So the rock has the Earth's magnetic field 'frozen' into it at the time of its making.

Using sensitive devices called *magnetometers* geologists can measure the strength and direction of this *palaeo-magnetism* ('magnetism from the past').

Palaeomagnetism gives us a lot of information about the Earth's history. For example, in different rocks the palaeomagnetic fields point in different directions. Now this could be due to two things. Either the magnetic North and South Poles have moved about through the ages as layers of rock formed one on top of another. Or the rocks were in a different place or facing a different direction when they were formed, and have since moved. In fact, both answers are true. The magnetic Poles have wandered in the past, and they are still doing so today, by a few inches each year. But the continents have also drifted and twisted so that their rocks face in different directions. Palaeomagnetism is strong scientific evidence for the idea of continental drift, which you can read more about on page 8.

## Back to front

As if all this wasn't complicated enough, scientists have discovered that the Earth's magnetic field is getting weaker by about 6 per cent every 100 years. Looking back through the magnetic record in the rocks, we find that many times the magnetic field has faded away and then it has become stronger again – but the other way round, with the South Pole where the North Pole was! These 'reversals' take from 2,000 to 10,000 years.

What with wandering poles, drifting continents, magnetic reversals and the magnetism of the past 'frozen' into rocks when they formed, our magnetic Earth certainly gives us some difficult puzzles to solve!

## A down-to-Earth magnetic field

You can make a 'picture' of the Earth's magnetic field using a small bar magnet, some iron filings, and a drawing of the Earth on a piece of paper.

Draw your Earth with its diameter about twice the length of the bar magnet. Put the magnet under the paper, tilted slightly from the Earth's true (geographic) North-South axis. Then sprinkle iron filings evenly over the paper and tap it gently. The filings will arrange themselves along the lines of magnetic force. If you have a small compass you can see how it too lines up with the magnetic field when placed in various positions near the Earth.

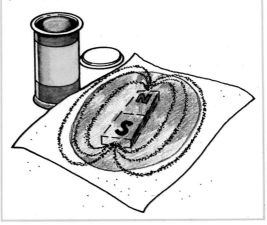

Do you know which way your house is facing? Or whether your garden points north or south? One way to find out is to make your own compass like the one shown here. You can then use it in the project on page 13.

*Project*

## A crafty compass!

To make your compass you will need a small, circular tin can (preferably with a lid), a cork, three steel needles, some cardboard, a bar magnet and a pen, scissors and some glue.

## *Step 1*

Remove the lid of your can and make sure it is clean inside. Then glue the cork to the bottom of the can, making sure it is in the center. Stick one of the needles into the cork so it too is standing upright in the center of the can and level with the top.

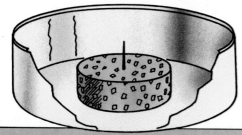

## *Step 2*

You now need to magnetize your other two needles. To do this, stroke them with the magnet, one at a time, always moving from the needle's eye to its point. You will soon find that they have become magnetic. This is because the pull of the magnet will rearrange the atoms making up the needles so that they all face the same way. Their south poles will be at the point and their north pole at the eye.

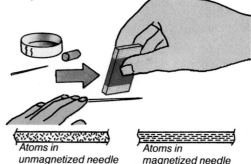

Atoms in unmagnetized needle

Atoms in magnetized needle

## *Step 3*

Cut a circle out of the cardboard that is just smaller than the circumference of the can and make a round hole in its middle, about ⅜ in (1 cm) across. This will be your compass card. Now cut a small strip of cardboard about 1⅛ in (3 cms) long and wide enough to fit snugly into the center hole of the compass card. This will be your pivot card.

Now carefully divide the cardboard circle into four equal sections. Mark each line with the directions North, South, East and West, being careful to get them in the right order (as in the picture below).

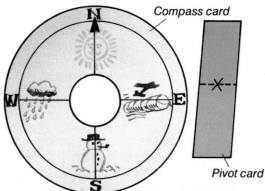

Compass card

Pivot card

## Step 4

Stick the two magnetized needles on to the bottom of the cardboard circle, either side of the pivot hole as shown. Make sure that both the eyes are pointing south and both the points are pointing north. The poles of the needles will be attracted to the opposite poles of the Earth.

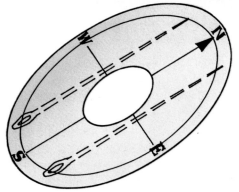

## Step 5

Now fold the pivot card in half and tuck it into the center hole of the compass card. Then balance the whole thing on the upright needle in the can. The magnetic pull from the Earth will cause the needles to swing around until they are facing north. Now you can work out which way your house is facing just by standing in front of it with your compass in your hand! Remember to replace the can's lid when carrying your compass about.

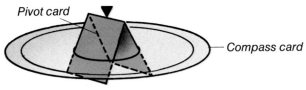

*Pivot card*

*Compass card*

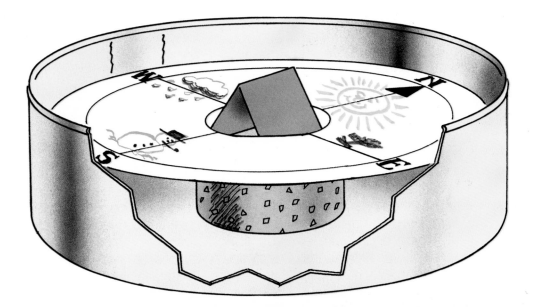

# A WORLD OF ROCK

**D**ig down anywhere on Earth and you'll hit solid rock. Rocks are the building material for the Earth's crust. And beneath the crust is more rock – the magma, or molten rock, of the mantle layer.

But what exactly is a rock? Different scientists would give you different descriptions, or at least, different parts of the same description. A mineralogist, for example, would tell you that all rocks are made from minerals. So what is a mineral? It is a naturally-occurring substance with a certain chemical make-up. Many minerals are made of two or more *elements* combined to form molecules of a *compound*. Calcium and carbon and oxygen, for instance, combine to form molecules of chalk (which a chemist would give the formula $CaCO_3$). This is a very soft, white mineral. Other minerals are made of just one element. Pure metals, sulphur, and diamond (which consists of only carbon) come into this group. All in all there are about 2,000 minerals. The most important ones in the Earth's crust are made of silicon, aluminum, iron and magnesium combined in various ways with oxygen.

A microscopist, on the other hand, might place more emphasis on the fact that, in the average lump of rock, minerals form crystals. This happens when atoms or molecules of a mineral line up in a certain pattern to create a regular shape such as a cube or some other many-faced solid. If you could take a slice of rock, grind it to wafer-thinness and then look at it under the microscope, you would see a complicated 3-D jigsaw of these crystals. Sometimes you can see

crystals without a microscope – 'precious stones' like emeralds or rubies, for example, or even the mineral crystals you sprinkle on your chips which are really tiny cubes of sodium chloride (salt).

The crystallographer takes this aspect of rocks into great detail. By passing X-rays through minerals, and by many

*Not far beneath the surface soil lie the rocks that make up the Earth's crust. Each layer of this sandstone rock in Cedar Beech National Park, California, USA, is distinctive because it contains a slightly different combination of minerals.*

other scientific tests, he can deduce the pattern of molecules inside the crystal, and tell you which elements are present and how they are combined.

Finally there is the geologist who puts all these different sciences together. He is interested in the minerals in the rock, in its crystal structure, and also in its physical properties such as density, hardness, color and shinyness. He could probably make a good guess at where a particular type of rock comes from and how long ago it was formed. But he would probably call in all his expert colleagues to check that his answers were correct!

# ROCKS OF AGES

There are literally thousands of different rock types on the Earth, but geologists divide them into three groups depending on how they were formed. These groups are called *igneous* rocks, *sedimentary* rocks, and *metamorphic* rocks. Like everything else about the Earth, our rocks are not still. The sun-powered weathering and erosion that takes place on the surface (see page 28), plus the heat coming from deep inside the Earth, combine to keep rocks moving and changing from one type to another in what is called the 'rock cycle'.

On the Earth's surface there are plenty of rocks from all three groups. However, deep underground the rocks are mainly of the igneous type. In fact, over nine-tenths of the Earth's crust is made up of igneous rocks.

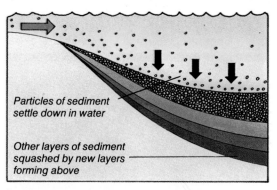

Particles of sediment settle down in water

Other layers of sediment squashed by new layers forming above

## Sedimentary rocks

These are made from particles of sediment like those that make up sand, silt and mud. Sedimentary means 'settling down' and as these particles collect and settle over hundreds and thousands of years, they form a thick, heavy layer that becomes squashed into solid rock by more particles collecting above. So sedimentary rocks are usually found in layers. Unless the layers have been disturbed by Earth movements (see page 26), the oldest rocks will be at the bottom and the youngest ones at the top. Around three-quarters of the rocks at the Earth's surface are sedimentary. In general, they are not as hard as the rocks in the other two groups. Limestone, clay, chalk and coal are all examples of sedimentary rocks.

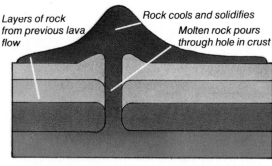

Layers of rock from previous lava flow

Rock cools and solidifies

Molten rock pours through hole in crust

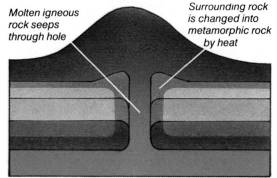

Molten igneous rock seeps through hole

Surrounding rock is changed into metamorphic rock by heat

## Igneous rocks

Igneous means 'fiery', so you might guess that igneous rocks are formed when rock melts under great temperatures and then solidifies again. The molten rock far below the surface is called *magma*. Sometimes it squirts out through holes in the Earth's crust that we call volcanoes, and then we call the molten rock *lava*.

As you can imagine, it needs to be very hot to melt rock. The various solid crystals in the rock turn into liquid depending on the melting temperature of the minerals they are made from. Granite is a well-known igneous rock that melts at about 800°C.

## Metamorphic rocks

Metamorphic means 'changed in shape or form'. So you won't be surprised to discover that metamorphic rocks are rocks that have been changed by the great temperatures and pressures in the Earth's crust. For example, a sedimentary rock buried to an enormous depth would be changed into a metamorphic rock by the huge weight of the rocks above. Or the high temperature of an igneous rock seeping into a crack could turn the rocks on either side into metamorphic ones. Marble, slate and quartzite are all metamorphic rocks.

*Under the microscope, fantastic colors and shapes are revealed in a slice of lava from Mount Vesuvius. The patterns are formed by the different mineral crystals that make up this igneous rock.*

## Starting from scratch

When identifying minerals and the rocks that contain them, it helps to know how hard they are. The laboratory geologist has complex machines to give accurate values for hardness, but out on expeditions the field geologist needs something more rough-and-ready. He uses instead the Mohs scale of hardness, invented by 1812 by Friedrich Mohs, an Austrian mineralogist.

On the scale, a substance is given a hardness score of between 1 and 10, depending on whether it scratches, or is scratched by, the standard minerals of the scale. For instance, if mineral X scratches a piece of quartz but not a topaz, its hardness is around 7½. Geologists don't always carry the full set of 10 standard minerals around with them, so they use handy things like fingernails, whose hardness they also know, to get a rough estimate.

| Mineral | Hardness | Handy helpers |
|---|---|---|
| Talc | 1 | |
| Gypsum | 2 | |
| | | Fingernail 2½ |
| Calcite | 3 | Copper coin 3 |
| Fluorite | 4 | |
| Apatite | 5 | Steel knife blade 5 |
| Orthoclase | 6 | Glass just less than 6 |
| Quartz | 7 | Hardened steel file 7 |
| Topaz | 8 | |
| Corundum | 9 | |
| Diamond | 10 | Hardest natural substance; 90 times harder than No 9 |

# USEFUL MINERALS

Everywhere you look you can see minerals. Some of them may have been taken from the Earth and cut and polished into precious stones like rubies or emeralds. Others may serve a more practical purpose. Diamonds, for example, aren't only used to make expensive jewelry. You'll also find them in many sorts of drill bits, being used to cut through rocks in mines or above oil wells, and they are also used to form the 'needle' on some record players!

*These sparkling gems from deep in the Earth are both forms of corundum which is an extremely*

**Gold** has been one of our most precious minerals since the beginning of civilization. It is easy to work, does not tarnish and is prized for its beauty. Apart from jewelry and ornaments, gold is used for filling teeth, and in the making of electrical circuits and solar cells carried by spacecraft.

**Pyrite** (also known as iron pyrites or fool's gold) is often mistaken for gold but is much harder and tarnishes easily. It gives off sparks when struck and is sometimes used instead of flint in lighters.

**Feldspar** comes in many forms and is the commonest mineral of all, making up about 60% of the Earth's crust. Feldspar crystals vary greatly in size – from tiny examples to ones that measure several yards across. One of its uses is in the making of china.

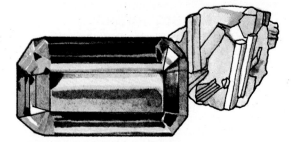

**Beryl** comes in several varieties. It is usually green and we know its purest crystals by their common name of emeralds. It is commonly found in a special form of granite called pegmatite but also occurs in ordinary granite and surrounding metamorphic rocks.

*The blue and yellow ones are sapphires and the red ones, are rubies.*

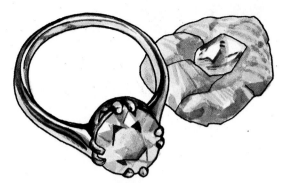

**Diamond** is the hardest natural substance on the Earth, yet it is made of the same element (carbon) as the soft black soot that collects in your chimney. Pure diamonds are colorless but colored varieties are sometimes found. Only a small proportion of diamonds are good enough to be cut into the familiar gems found in rings and other jewelry. The rest are used for a variety of jobs. They are the only substance that can be used to cut other diamonds.

**Quartz** is another common mineral in the Earth's crust. It comes in many different forms – like amethyst, rock crystal and tiger's eye – and lots of different colors. It is often used to imitate diamonds in rings and other jewelry and, in its various forms, is used in electronic watches, the making of sandpaper and various optical instruments.

**Sulphur** (also known as brimstone) easily catches fire and produces strong fumes of sulphur dioxide. It is used to make matches and gunpowder in fireworks and its bright yellow color is used to make dye.

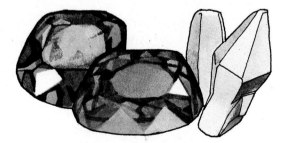

**Corundum** is the hardest natural substance after diamond and comes in many forms. Rubies and sapphires are well-known varieties of this mineral and it is also used to make emery (for filing nails!) and bearings inside watches.

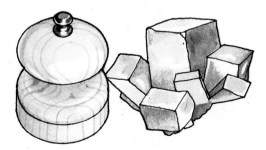

**Salt** is a crystal form of the mineral known as halite. It forms tiny cubes which you can see if you look at a sprinkling of table salt under a magnifying glass. Salt is very important as a food preservative. It also melts ice and is spread on icy roads during winter.

# WHAT ROCK IS THAT?

Is your house built of brick or stone? What about the other buildings in your area — are any of them made out of local rock? Now look at the roofs. You will probably find that most of them are covered with dark grey slates or red clay tiles. All of these building materials originally came from rocks buried in the Earth's crust. For many years man has dug away at the ground, extracting minerals and rocks to use in his everyday life. Here you can see some examples of different rock types.

## IGNEOUS ROCKS

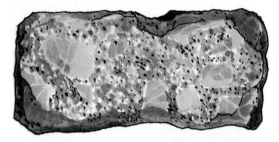

**Granite** solidifies slowly below ground, so its crystals are fairly large (²/₁₀ in [5 mm] or more across). It is a very hard rock containing mainly quartz and feldspar.

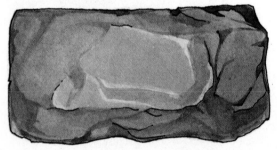

**Basalt** is solidified lava and is the main rock of the sea bed. Its small crystals are made up of mainly plagioclase, pyroxene and magnetite.

**Obsidian** cools so quickly that crystals do not have time to grow. Instead it looks like lumps of black glass.

## SEDIMENTARY ROCKS

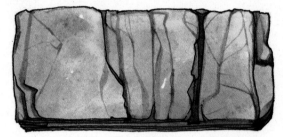

**Shale** is a soft rock made from loosely-packed mud. It consists mainly of clay minerals (various mixtures of aluminum, silicon and oxygen). It is laid down in thin layers and will crack or flake easily along these lines, which are known as *fissure planes*.

*All rocks are made of minerals. This slice through a lump of rock shows the mineral crystals of*

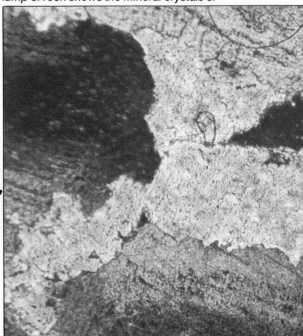

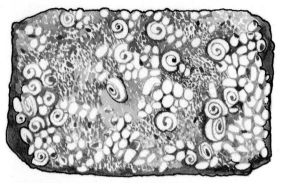

Limestone is made mainly of calcium carbonate, like chalk. It often contains the shells of many sea creatures.

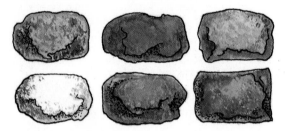

Sandstone is a crumbly rock made of rounded grains of compacted sand (quartz). It forms under seas and deserts and, like shale, it may contain fossils.

*limestone (orange) and dolomite (grey) which are often found together.*

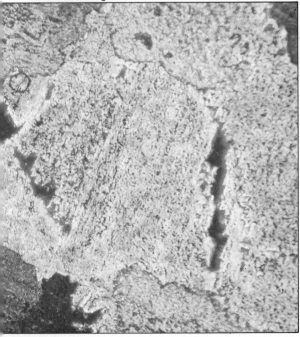

# METAMORPHIC ROCKS

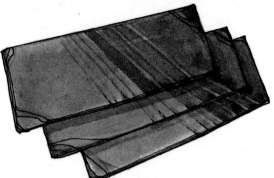

Slate is a dark, fine-grained rock that splits into sheets. It is formed by tremendous heat and pressure acting on shales and mudstones.

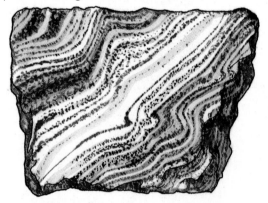

Gneiss contains bands of light and dark color. It is formed when the original rock becomes so hot that it almost melts and the crystals can move and collect in colored layers.

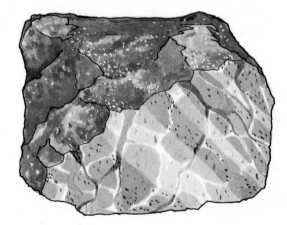

Marble is a sparkly, sugar-looking rock that we can polish into a glass-like, glossy finish. It is formed by great heat acting on limestones.

We are surrounded by rocks and minerals, not only in their natural forms but also by the many articles into which they're made. The china mug that holds your morning cocoa is made from clay. The glass that forms a window starts off as quartz sand. And all the metals that go into making a bike were originally extracted from ore minerals deep in the ground.

This might begin to give you an idea of how important rocks and minerals are in our lives. You might like to start making a list, or even a collection, of some of the things we turn rocks and minerals into. It is also fun to go out looking for rocks and minerals in their natural state and make these into your own personal collection as well.

## Project 2

## Making a rock and mineral collection

Before you go out collecting rocks and minerals, you first need to collect together some equipment. You will need your *Science Notebook,* a pen and pencil, some sticky labels, some newspaper and a carrier bag. A geological hammer would also be useful for splitting rocks and pebbles. These are specially made so that they will not break up when hammering hard rocks. To mount your collection at home you will need a shallow box or drawer, some felt clay and more sticky labels.

### Step 1

First of all you need to find out a bit about the *geology* of your area – in other words the local rock types. You can often tell a lot simply by looking at old houses in your neighbourhood. If lots of them are made from limestone or granite, for example, then this may have been dug out of a nearby quarry. If there is a museum in your area, then try to visit it. There may be an exhibit showing local rocks and minerals, even fossils, which will give you a good idea of what to look for and where, as well as providing information on what the different types of rock and mineral look like.

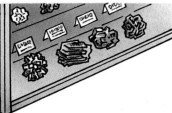

### Step 2

Now look at a large scale map of your area or, if possible, try to get hold of a geological map which will show the distribution and age of the local rocks. The best places to look for rocks and minerals are quarries, cliffs, mine dumps and road and railway cuttings, although any rocky outcrop could prove interesting. River beds and banks, beaches and building sites are other good places to look.

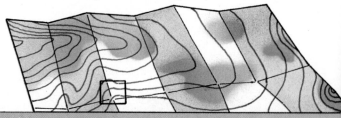

## Golden rules for good scientists

Before you set out to explore any of these places, remember to take the following safety precautions:

**1** Always tell someone where you are going and take a parent or friend with you.

**2** Always get permission to visit quarries or dumps, or any sites that are on private land.

**3** Be very careful when exploring cliffs or other rocky outcrops. Watch the tides if you're on the beach otherwise you may find yourself stranded, and never try to climb onto dangerous ledges.

**4** Try not to hammer rocks to loosen specimens unless absolutely necessary. Many samples can be loosened by hand or found simply lying on the ground. Remember, hammering speeds up erosion and usually leaves an ugly scar on the rocks.

**5** If you have to hammer rocks, do so on the ground, not against the rock face. Remember to hold one hand in front of your face or wear some protective glasses in case any chips of rock fly up and hit you.

*Step 3* Use a good guide book to identify any rocks or minerals that you find. Then label each one with its name and the place where it was found, wrap it carefully in newspaper and put it in the carrier bag. Make any extra notes in your *Science Notebook*.

*Step 4* When you get home, take each specimen in turn and remove its label. Then carefully wash it in warm soapy water to remove any loose dust and dirt. Of course, you should first check that your sample is not going to dissolve as soon as you immerse it in water. In other words, make sure it is not *soluble*.

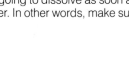

*Step 5* Leave each sample to dry while you prepare the shallow box or drawer that will house your collection. Line it with felt or tissue paper, and then place your finds neatly on it, holding them in place with some clay. Write out a new label to stick beside each sample with its name and all the other information you have recorded.

# BENDS AND BREAKS

**R**ocks are so solid, hard and brittle that it is difficult to imagine them bending or folding. But all over the world huge slabs of rock, hundreds of miles across, are being folded like pieces of paper or torn like slices of bread by the gigantic forces from within the Earth.

If a slab or plate of rock is squashed at the sides, it may react in various ways. It may bend upwards into a dome shape. (This can also happen if magma wells up beneath the slab and forces it upwards.) Or it may fold in one or more places, forming 'waves' in the rock that we call mountains and valleys. It may even snap to produce a *fault*. One fault edges then rides over the other as the squashing continues. A rock slab that is being stretched may also snap, to create a deep rift valley.

All this bending and breaking usually takes a long time – thousands of millions of years. But occasionally things happen much faster. A crack may appear in a few minutes as the ground shakes and the rock is torn apart by an earthquake. Or lava can erupt from within the Earth and build a new mountain in just a few days.

All these processes cover the Earth with hills, valleys, mountains, scars, cracks, domes, basins and many other *topographical* features. The ripples and folds do not remain for ever, though. Forces from within the Earth create the ups and downs of our landscape, but forces from without – the Sun, wind, rain and ice – are always at the ready to rub away the mountains and fill up the valleys, as you can read on page 28.

*Gigantic pressure within the Earth forces surface rocks into the shapes xxxx xxx mountains. Here the distant skyline of the Sierra Nevada Mountains in the USA illustrates the jagged, rippling result of geographical movement and erosion.*

## BIG IS BEAUTIFUL!

▶ The biggest single rock in the world is Mount Augustus in Western Australia. It is 5 miles (8 kms) long and 2 miles (3 kms) wide.

▶ The highest point on Earth is Mount Everest which is 29,028 feet (8,848 meters) above sea level. This 5½ mile peak was eventually conquered in 1953 by Edmund Hilary and Tenzing Norgay, but only after 11 people had lost their lives trying to reach the top.

▶ The world's tallest mountain is Mauna Kea in Hawaii which measures 33,476 feet (10,023 meters), although 25,727 feet (7,718 meters) are hidden below the sea.

# SHAPING THE LAND

Forces from within the Earth are continually bulging and buckling the crust to create mountains and valleys. But what about the forces from outside? At the same time, the natural forces at the Earth's surface are fighting back – trying to known down the mountains, fill in the valleys and generally wear down the lumps and bumps. These forces are all, in one way or another, driven by the Sun.

## Heat

Rocks are not very good at withstanding heat and cold. If you heated a rock up, then cooled it down, then heated it again, and so on, it would soon start to break up. Rocks expand in the heat and contract in the cold, and this causes cracks to appear and bits to fall off. So as the Sun beats down during the day and then disappears during the cold of the night, rocks all over the world are cracking and breaking and being worn away.

## Water

The Sun also provides heat that evaporates water from rivers, lakes and seas. The water vapor rises up into the air and condenses to form clouds. Eventually it turns to rain that beats down on the soil and rock, dissolving it and rubbing it away.

The rainwater then collects in rivers which rush over their stony beds, gouging grooves out of the rock and wearing it down. As the fast currents slow down in lakes or estuaries, the particles they carry fall to the bottom as sediment, so that these areas gradually 'silt up', filling with mud and silt and other bits and pieces. And all along the coast waves whipped up by the wind are crashing against the land, wearing away the shoreline.

The Earth's surface rocks can be dramatically altered by the forces of weathering. Here, Angel

## Ice

As water crystallizes into ice it expands. So, when rainwater seeps into the tiny cracks that are always present on any rock's surface, it freezes during cold weather, expands and opens up the cracks. The rock is then weakened and chips fall off to expose new cracks beneath. The next rain shower fills them and so the process continues. More bits flake off until gradually even the hardest smoothest rock is worn away.

## Valley shapes

### Glacial erosion – U-valleys

Ice is a powerful weapon in the shaping of the landscape. This can be seen very clearly in a glacier, which is basically a river of frozen water moving slowly but surely down to the sea. As the ice 'flows', it picks up stones that rub away at the surrounding soil and rock, grinding away a steep-sided, U-shaped valley.

These glacier valleys are common all over the Earth – not just where it's very cold. This is because, at some times in the past, the Earth was much colder than it is now and glaciers were much more common. Also, some continents have drifted near the Poles during their history and so it was cold enough for glaciers to form on them.

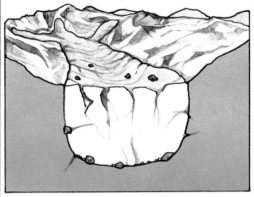

### River erosion – V-valleys

The steeper a hill or mountain, the faster water flows down its sides. This water eventually collects to form a river which picks up boulders and stones during its journey and whirls them along, carving holes and grooves in the rocks below. As the river cuts deeper into the ground, lumps of rock at the top are undercut and fall into the river. Gradually the valley created by this river erosion deepens and widens into a V-shape.

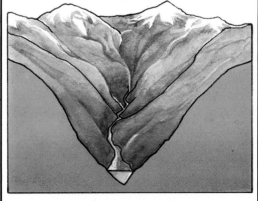

*Arch in Utah, USA, shows the extraordinary effects of wind erosion*

## A flat Earth?

If you look back at all these processes, you'll see that there is an awful lot of wearing-away going on. Water, wind, rain and ice are at work day and night, all over the world, trying to level our landscape. These forces are together called *weathering and erosion*. In the titanic battle between Earth and Sun, the Earth keeps making new mountains and valleys while the Sun-powered forces of erosion keep trying to flatten them.

# BENEATH THE SURFACE

Erosion does not happen only on the Earth's surface. In countryside where the main rock layers are made of limestone, erosion is also going on beneath the surface. To understand why this happens, the all-around scientist needs to turn his inquiring mind to a little *geochemistry*...

## Dissolving the ground!

Limestone rocks are basically made up of calcium carbonate crystals (from the mineral calcite). They are fairly resistant to being dissolved in water – at least, in pure water. But rainwater is not pure. As raindrops fall through the air and seep through the soil, they dissolve tiny amounts of the carbon dioxide gas that is present in our atmosphere. This makes the rainwater into a weak acid called carbonic

acid. Now, it so happens that carbonic acid is very good at dissolving calcium carbonate crystals, turning them into calcium bicarbonate solution.

The result is that every shower of rain falling on a limestone area dissolves away a little part of the countryside. Even on a fairly smooth limestone surface the water soon widens the natural limestone joints into big cracks. This opens the way to large-scale underground erosion, as you can see in the picture on the right. On the surface there may be just a small pothole, but beneath there could be miles of tunnels, shafts and caves. With the passing of time so much limestone is dissolved away that the caves eventually collapse into a jumbled heap of rocks. Erosion has won again!

## Tunnels and caves

We have now mapped most of the Earth's surface – much of it by taking photographs from airplanes. But caves and tunnels are nowhere near as easy to map, and many large underground cave networks are probably still waiting to be discovered. For the time being...

▶ The biggest cave network in the world is under the Mammoth Cave National Park in Kentucky, USA. The total length of tunnels, caves and passageways is nearly 300 miles (over 470 kms).
▶ The largest single cave is the Sarawak Chamber in the Gunung Mulu Park, Sarawak. It is 700 meters long and 300 meters wide, on average, which is enough for over 75 football fields.
▶ The deepest cave is at Reseau de Foillis in the French Pyrenees. It goes down over 5,000 feet (1,500 meters). That a lot of rock above your head!

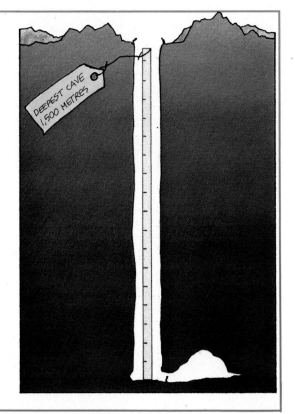

DEEPEST CAVE 1,500 METRES

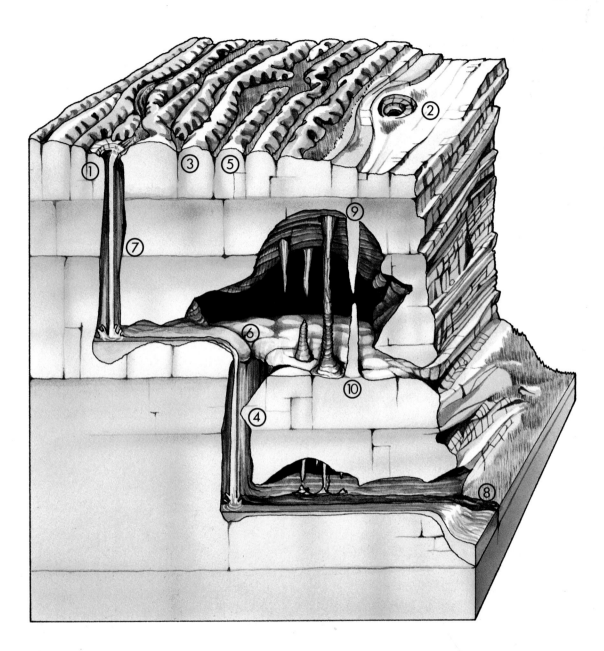

# KEY

**1 Sink-hole** or **swallow-hole** is where a stream disappears underground.

**2 Pot-hole** used to be a sink-hole but the stream has now altered its course to leave a simple hole in the ground.

**3 Grikes** are deep, narrow cracks in the limestone.

**4 Connecting sink** is where water eroded its way from one layer of limestone to the one beneath.

**5 Clints** are the blocks of limestone that occur between grikes.

**6 Caves** are carved out of the rock by running water, or floodwater.

**7 Chimneys** are shafts where the water falls deep into the limestone.

**8 Resurgence** is where the stream reappears after its journey through the caves and tunnels.

**9 Stalactites** are hanging stone points formed by water dangling from the roof of the cave and evaporating, leaving behind dissolved minerals.

**10 Stalagmites** are stone points formed by water dripping on to the floor of the cave and evaporating, leaving behind dissolved minerals.

# LIFE ON EARTH

**E**arth is only one of nine planets circling the Sun. Yet it alone (as far as we know) supports life. Many people say how amazed they are that the Earth happens to have exactly the right conditions for life. It receives just the right amounts of light and heat from the Sun. There is plenty of water, lots of air to breathe, and plenty of minerals for living things to use for their growth ... what a marvelous coincidence!

The scientist, however, is more thoughtful. He recognizes that this is not simply one big accident. It's no coincidence that the conditions here on Earth are suitable for our type of life. More sensibly, life on Earth has developed to fit in with the conditions that exist here, and the various plants and animals have learned to use the light, heat, water and minerals in the best way they can. Very probably there *is* life elsewhere in the universe; life that will have evolved to fit in with the conditions that exist on other planets. And, of course, these other forms of life may be so different from our own that we might not even recognize them as living beings at first!

In fact, only a tiny fraction of the Earth bears life. Living things cannot exist more than a few yards below the surface, or more than a few miles, above it. Given the size of the Earth, life occupies an incredibly thin 'skin' at its surface. This skin is called the *biosphere*.

The study of life itself takes us from earth science, geology and similar areas, into biology. However, the Earth's influence is never far away when we look at where plants and animals live, why they live there, and how they fit into

their surroundings.

The Earth also makes, stores, and occasionally reveals, treasures that help

us to look back at the history of life on Earth. These treasures help us to find out about how life first appeared and how and why it has changed in the past. They are called *fossils,* and you can read about them on the next page.

**33**

# ROCK RECORD

For many centuries great scientists and thinkers argued about fossils. What were they? How were they formed, and when? What could they tell us about the Earth? Not surprisingly, different people came up with conflicting answers to all these questions. During the Middle Ages some learned people believed that fossils were not, as we now know, the remains of once-living plants and animals. Instead, they thought they were types of mineral, like gemstones, made by the Earth's natural rock-forming processes. Others recognized that some fossils were so similar to some of the

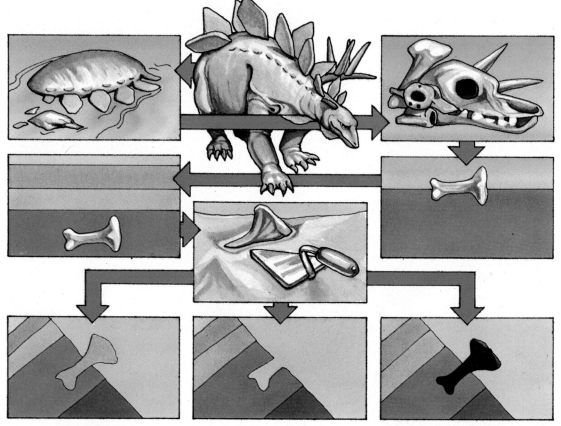

*Mineralized fossil*                    *Mould fossil*                    *Cast fossil*

## How fossils form

Here you can see how fossils form. If the remains are dug up unchanged they form a *mineralized* fossil. If they dissolve away, they leave a hole called a *mould* fossil. If this hole becomes filled with other minerals, it is called a *cast* fossil.

*1 An animals dies and its remains are washed onto mud or clay under shallow water at a riverbank.*
*2 The flesh quickly rots away, leaving only hard parts such as bones or teeth.*

*3 The hard parts are soon covered by sediment which creates layers as more mud collects on top.*
*4 Over many years the bones and teeth absorb minerals from the surrounding substance. Gradually they turn to stone. The layers of mud deepen until the lower ones are eventually squeezed to form sedimentary rock.*
*5 Earth movements over millions of years shift the layers of rock to create new mountains or deep ravines and erosion wears them away so that their fossil treasures are uncovered.*

plants and animals still living on the Earth that they could not be 'accidents of nature'. They had to be *organic remains* – the remains of living things somehow buried in the rocks and changed to stone.

Some fossils were quite different from today's creatures and once again the scientist's inquiring mind wanted to know: why? Those who followed the Bible said that every so often God became displeased with the Earth. He ordered worldwide catastrophes such as the Great Flood for which Noah built his Ark. Each catastrophe swept away all life, and God created a new and improved set of plants and animals to live on the empty Earth.

Some people did not accept this view. There was no way it could be tested scientifically and, anyway, once you started explaining things by 'God's will' then you could explain away almost anything.

## The real reason

In the 1800's some geologists, naturalists and *palaeontologists* (fossil experts) began looking for a more scientific explanation. One of these was a man called Sir Charles Lyell. Along with others, he argued that the same processes we shaping our world today – such as erosion, volcanoes and mountain-building earth movements – have always been at work on our planet. These natural processes are enough to account for the changes we find in the rocks as well as the fossils they contain. He believed that the Earth is always changing, with some parts forming as others are destroyed, in a never-ending cycle. This is the view that most scientists accept today.

Another great scientist was impressed by Lyell's views. He traveled the world in the 1830's collecting animals, plants and fossils, and he wondered how living things had changed over time. His answers were to change the world of science for ever. His name was Charles Darwin.

# Science in action

## What fossils tell us

Some rocks, like limestone, are made up of many fossils. These plant and animal remains from our past can help scientists, like geologists and palaeontologists, in a number of ways.

A rock sample can be identified and dated (given a time when it was formed) depending on the fossils it contains. This helps to date other rocks above and below the fossil-containing layers, even if they do not contain fossils themselves. Of course, scientists can also do this the other way round – by guessing how old the fossils are from the types of rock they are found in. The whole dating business is, in fact, a two-way discussion between geologists and palaeontologists who fit rocks and fossils into one time scale.

Suppose today two regions of the Earth are far apart, yet the contain the same types of rock in the same order and thickness of layers. Scientists now know that it was possible, at some time in the past, for the two regions to have been joined together. And if they contain exactly the same types of fossil as well, then this is further evidence for the join. Such findings have been used to support the idea of *continental drift* – the theory that the plates supporting the land masses have moved about during the Earth's history. For instance, West Africa and eastern South America have many rocks and fossils in common. Their edges also fit quite neatly together. This makes scientists think that the two countries were once joined, until about 130 million years ago.

# WHAT LIVES WHERE

Even the most unobservant person knows that life does not cover the Earth's entire surface. Some parts are too cold, such as the Poles and the highest mountains, and some parts are too dry, such as the great deserts. However, life has a hold almost everywhere else and there is one scientist – the biogeographer – who studies this life, looking at which plants and animals live where, and why.

The Earth's biosphere can be divided into large regions called *biomes*. You can see the dozen or so main types of biome on the map below. Each biome is described by a certain type of plant or plants that live there. This is because plants are the basis for all life on Earth. Without plants the herbivores (plant-eating animals) would have no food and so would die. And without them, the carnivores (meat-eaters) would also die. (In fact, you could say that all life on Earth is plant-powered!)

## Making the best of it!

In each biome, plants have adapted to make the best of the conditions found there

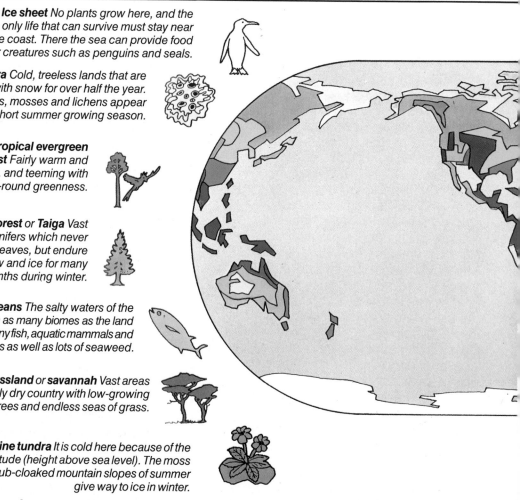

***Ice sheet*** *No plants grow here, and the only life that can survive must stay near the coast. There the sea can provide food for creatures such as penguins and seals.*

***Tundra*** *Cold, treeless lands that are covered with snow for over half the year. Small flowers, mosses and lichens appear during the short summer growing season.*

***Subtropical evergreen forest*** *Fairly warm and wet, and teeming with life in year-round greenness.*

***Boreal forest*** *or* ***Taiga*** *Vast tracts of conifers which never lose their leaves, but endure snow and ice for many months during winter.*

***Seas and oceans*** *The salty waters of the Earth contain as many biomes as the land – home for many fish, aquatic mammals and other creatures as well as lots of seaweed.*

***Tropical grassland*** *or* ***savannah*** *Vast areas of hot and fairly dry country with low-growing acacia trees and endless seas of grass.*

***Alpine tundra*** *It is cold here because of the high altitude (height above sea level). The moss and scrub-cloaked mountain slopes of summer give way to ice in winter.*

– the temperature, rainfall, soil type, winds, and so on. For example, the pine and fir trees of the northern coniferous forests are built to withstand the long, cold winters of that region. Their bark is thick and tough and their leaves are small and needle-like, so that they can conserve water without freezing up. What's more, their leaves stay on all year round, so that they can make the most of the weak spring and autumn sunshine.

## A never-ending cycle

Everywhere that living things grow, they change the face of the Earth. Tree roots grow into cracks in stones and rocks, breaking them into smaller pieces and so helping with the wearing-away process of erosion. Animals do the same, by digging in the ground for food or tunneling for homes. Bits of dead animals and plants collect along with rock fragments in sedimentary layers that eventually become rock once again, and so the cycle continues.

One animal in particular has changed large areas of the Earth's surface beyond recognition, and interrupted the natural cycles of building and breaking down. This animal destroys whole forests, pushes back the sea by making dykes, and digs enormous quantities of minerals and other substances from the crust. You can read about this animal – the human – on page 38.

**Tropical rain forest** *Giant trees live in the year-long, warm dampness of these forests. They provide food and shelter for the richest collection of plants and animals to be found on the Earth.*

**Temperate grassland** *Variously called prairie, steppe and pampas. The grasses support large herds of grazing animals.*

**Temperate deciduous forest** *Leaves fall in autumn and much life remains dormant during the cold of winter until it is revived by the warmth of spring.*

**Semidesert** *Possibly cold, probably hot, but always dry. Life here is a struggle for the prickly cacti and other drought-resistant plants.*

**Desert** *The driest regions on Earth. Life is sparse or non-existent except after a rare rainshower.*

**Chaparral** or **scrub** *Mostly warm and dry. The main plants are tough, thorny bushes and low trees that can withstand both long droughts and being grazed by various animals.*

# THE EARTH EXPLOITED

**B**iologists and other life scientists see that, in the natural world, there is a continuous recycling of nutrients and minerals. Living things grow and die and their remains are returned to the Earth. Light energy from the Sun, captured by green plants and passed on to animals, is the power for life. If certain plants or animals become too numerous they run out of food or living space and their numbers fall back to a level that their surroundings can support. Like the Earth, nature takes care of itself.

Since we humans came on the scene, however, things have changed. We are so numerous and we need so much food that huge areas of forest are felled to make way for farmland to provide us with more to eat. But the forest soil, being thin, grows only a few crops before it becomes exhausted. Without the tree roots to bind it together, it soon becomes loose and easily washed away by rain. The land ends up bare and useless.

We also mine the Earth for metals, gems and other materials. We bore miles of tunnels and blast away whole mountains in search of the minerals that our modern society 'needs'. Quarries and spoil-heaps of left-over material scar the landscape. The mined materials are used to make cars and machinery that are thrown away after a few years and pile up into heaps of their own, while the factories that made them pour out polluting chemicals into the air and water.

We also burn *fossil fuels* (see page 40) at an enormous rate – far faster than they can be replaced. Oils and petroleums are turned into plastics and other materials

that are not biodegradable and so will not be destroyed naturally like the plants and animals from which they originally came. The plastic bottles washed up on the beach should remind us all of how polluted our world has become.

Scientists are partly responsible for the mess we are making of the Earth. Research continues to produce new killer

*An oil production platform looms out of the North Sea. The oil it extracts from deep beneath the sea bed is one of the Earth's major fossil fuels – and we use it faster than it can be replaced. (Inset) Open cast mining also alters the landscape – for ever.*

chemicals, dangerous substances such as radioactive wastes, and yet more ways of burning up our fuel reserves. But many scientists now realize that, although the Earth is big, it has its limits. We cannot carry on plundering our planet for ever. Supplies of minerals and fuels will eventually become too difficult to obtain, and there will be no more land suitable for farming. The time to act is now. We need to plan for the future by finding more efficient ways of using fuels and cleaner ways of farming, manufacturing goods, and being transported from place to place. Scientists have key roles in helping to safeguard the future, not only of our own species, but also of the entire planet.

# DIG AND DRILL

What's the most valuable substance in the world today? Gold? Or a precious gem such as a diamond? Perhaps, but there is also another substance that we take from the Earth which is so valuable that it has often been called 'black gold'. People who own the land under which it is found have become incredibly rich and hold great power. The substance is, of course, oil.

Oil comes in many forms which are better known to geologists as natural petroleums. They can be very thick, almost solid, like bitumen, or syrupy and sticky like tar, or more runny and liquid like the rock oils which are known as 'crude'.

Oil has so many uses that it would take a book much bigger than this one to describe them all. Most petroleum oils are taken from natural wells deep in the ground and pumped or transported by tanker to a refinery. This is a giant factory where the oils are heated, vaporized, cooled, condensed and mixed with chemicals in order to separate the crude into its many different parts. These parts include heating oils for burning; petrol and diesel to fuel cars, trucks and trains; kerosene for aircraft; oil bases for sealants and paints; tars and bitumens for road-making and building; plus raw materials that are used to make the hundreds of plastics and polyethylenes we find in almost everything from ballpens to the Space Shuttle...

Besides oil, coal and natural gas are also valuable materials that we take from the Earth. Coal is burned to generate electricity or to melt metals out of the solid rocks (ores) in which they are found. Gas is also burned to provide heat in furnaces, factories, offices and homes.

Oil, coal and gas took millions of years to form, but we are using them up in tens of years. True, the total amount of coal in the Earth's crust is vast, but it will gradually become more difficult to obtain. In the end, the amount of power needed to get the coal out will become bigger than the energy in the coal. This is why so many scientists are

## Fossil fuels from the Earth

**Oil** is found in rocks that once formed the beds of ancient seas. The tiny bodies of dead sea creatures fell to the ocean floors and partly decayed as layers of sedimentary rocks built up. Under great temperatures and pressures the animals remains became oil. Earth movements tilted some of these layers and transported them to places that are no longer under the sea, or the seas retreated so that other oil-bearing rocks are no longer under water.

Natural **gas** is trapped within the Earth's crust, usually in tiny holes in sponge-like rock. Gas is formed in two main ways. One is from petroleum oil heated to over 290°F (150°C) deep beneath the ground. This is why gas

## How oil and gas are formed

In prehistoric times the remains of tiny dead animals collected on the sea bed as a thick, rich mud. The mud built up in layers, hundreds of yards thick.

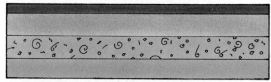

Over millions of years the remains became buried, heated, and pressurized. They changed into oil and gas inside the sedimentary rock that surrounded them.

Oil field        Gas field

Earth movements over time may have tilted the layers of rock and then new rock layers formed above them. Deep in the crust, the gas filtered through its rock layer, collecting as a giant 'bubble' below the impermeable rock. The oil remains as a 'pool' below it.

worried about a future 'energy crisis'. Today's young scientists will have vital work to do in tomorrow's world, ensuring that we save our mineral and energy supplies and use them in the most efficient ways.

is often found 'floating' above oil deposits in *porous* rocks. The other way gas forms is by chemical changes in the plant remains found scattered in sedimentary rocks. Coal forms in a similar way, which is why some gas pockets are also found in or near coal seams.

**Coal** was mostly formed during the *Carboniferous* period around 300 million years ago. At that time much of the Earth was warm and wet, and giant fern trees and other prehistoric plants grew quickly in the steamy swamps. The plant remains piled up in layers and gradually, as more remains and rocks collected on top of them, they were squashed into the organic black rock we call coal. Anthracite is the type of coal most often used in the home.

### How coal is formed

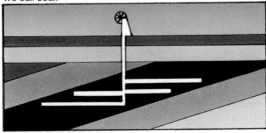

*About 200-300 millions years ago, thick layers of partly decomposed plant remains formed in the prehistoric swamps.*

*As more rocks formed on top, the plant-rich layers were compressed into the black, fossil-rich sedimentary rock we call coal.*

*To become good quality coal the layers must have at some time been buried 10,000 to 20,000 feet (3,000 to 6,000 meters) below the surface, though they may have been pushed upwards by Earth movements and erosion. In some cases coal is mined at the surface in what is called an open-cast mine.*

# Science in action

## Finding the Earth's riches

Experts from many branches of science work together to locate deposits of oil, coal, gas, and other valuable materials in the Earth's crust. Here are some of the methods they use.

**Rock types** Certain minerals are found in particular rocks. Geologists examine the rocks on the surface and also check whether the rock layers are tilted, and if so at which angle. Then, by making comparisons with similar rock layers, from other places, they can guess whether certain areas are likely to hold mineral wealth.

**Satellite photographs** By examining photographs taken from high above the Earth, scientists can identify particular rock formations and types of landscape. They use infra-red (heat) photos as well as ordinary light ones.

**Magnetic mapping** As explained on page 13, the magnetic properties of some rocks give clues, as to when they were formed and where. Also some rocks such as iron ores are themselves magnetic and so easily detected.

**Seismic recordings** The shock waves from earthquakes and volcanoes travel through the Earth at different speeds and directions depending on which material they pass through (see page 7). This gives seismologists many clues as to what is beneath the surface. Instead of waiting for a convenient earthquake, however, they usually set of small underground test explosions to generate the shock waves.

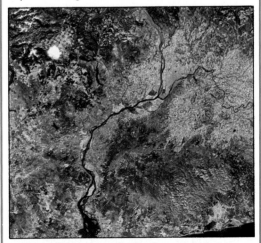

*In this satellite photograph of the Cascade Mountains different types of vegetation show up in different colors. Mount Saint Helens can be seen as a white dot, top left.*

# THINGS TO REMEMBER

## What the words mean....

Here are some explanations of words in this book that you may find unfamiliar. They aren't the exact scientific definitions, because many of these are extremely complicated, but the descriptions will help you to understand the STEP INTO SCIENCE books.

**ASTHENOSPHERE** The molten rock inside the Earth on which the plates of the lithosphere float.

**BIOMES** Different regions of the Earth that are characterized by certain types of plants.

**BIOSPHERE** A thin zone at the surface of the Earth, where all life exists.

**CONTINENTAL DRIFT** The movement of the continental plates across the surface of the Earth.

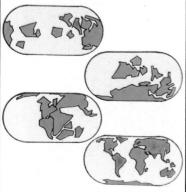

**CORE** The innermost part of the Earth.

**CRUST** A kind of 'skin' surrounding the Earth.

**DEEP-SEA TRENCH** A valley deep on the ocean floor.

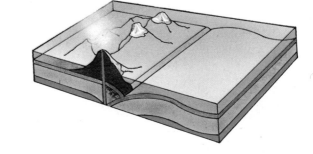

**EARTHQUAKE** Shock waves passing through the Earth's crust caused by the movement of plates.

**EROSION** The wearing away of the landscape by water, wind, rain and ice.

**FAULT** Where a plate of rock cracks or snaps and the two sides either drift apart or one rides over the other.

**FOSSILS** Plant and animal remains from the distant past.

**GEOLOGY** The study of rocks, minerals and their structure.

**GLACIER** A river of ice that moves slowly towards the sea, forming a valley as it goes.

**GUTENBERG DISCONTINUITY** Where the rocks of the Earth's mantle give way to the denser rocks of the core.

**IGNEOUS** A type of rock formed from rocks that have melted under great heat and/or pressure and then solidified again.

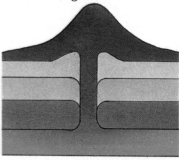

**LAVA** Molten rock from the magma that is forced out through holes or cracks in the crust.

**LITHOSPHERE** A layer of movable plates surrounding the Earth, made up of the crust and part of the mantle.

**MANTLE** A layer of the Earth that falls between the crust and the core.

**MAGMA** Molten, liquid rock far below the surface.

**METAMORPHIC** A type of rock that has been changed in form by great temperatures and pressures.

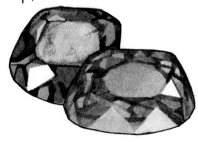

**MINERAL** A naturally-occurring substance with a characteristic chemical make up.

**MOHOROVICIC DISCONTINUITY** Where the lighter rocks of the crust give way to the heavier ones of the mantle.

**MOHS SCALE** A scale of hardness used to help identify minerals and the rocks that contain them.

**PALAEONTOLOGY** The study of fossils.

**PLATE TECTONICS** A theory that says the Earth's surface is made up of a series of plates which can move about.

**ROCK** Hard, compact substance that makes up much of the Earth and is made of minerals.

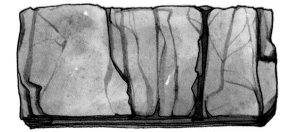

**SEDIMENT** Small particles of matter that collect, layer by layer, in water or on land to form rock.

**SEDIMENTARY** A type of rock made from sediment that has been squashed together under great pressure.

**SEISMOLOGY** A branch of science that is concerned with the study of earth movements and earthquakes.

**TRANSFORM FAULT** A boundary between two plates which simply slide past each other.

**VOLCANO** A cone of igneous rock through which molten rock escapes under great pressure.

**WEATHERING** The breaking up of rock on the Earth's surface by natural forces such as rain, sun and wind.